ROCKED

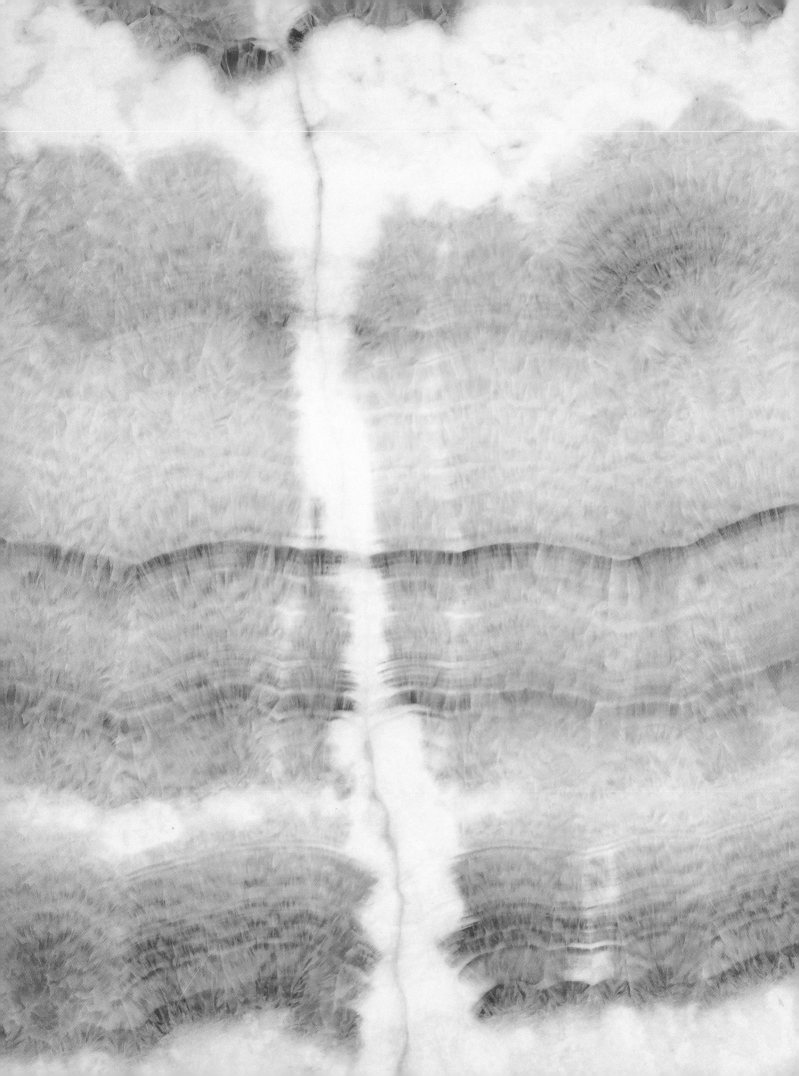

ROCKED

Interviews Part One

TANGUY VAN QUICKENBORNE
10

JOOST DECLERCQ
13

KASPER BOSMANS
14

DRIES VAN NOTEN
17

XAVIER HUFKENS
18

Chapters

CHAPTER ONE
21

CHAPTER TWO
69

CHAPTER THREE
119

CHAPTER FOUR
147

CHAPTER FIVE
185

Interviews Part Two

SEBASTIEN CAPORUSSO
242

FIEN MULLER
245

DRIES CRIEL
246

STEFAAN DE CROOCK
249

HANNES PEER
250

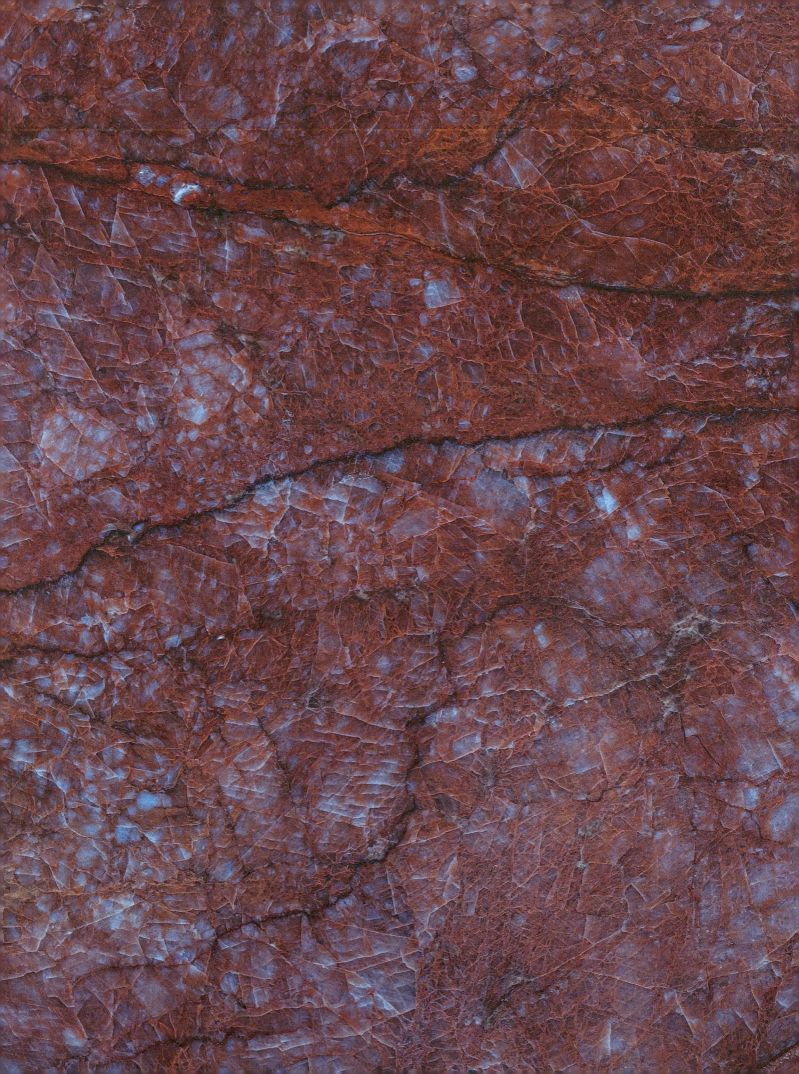

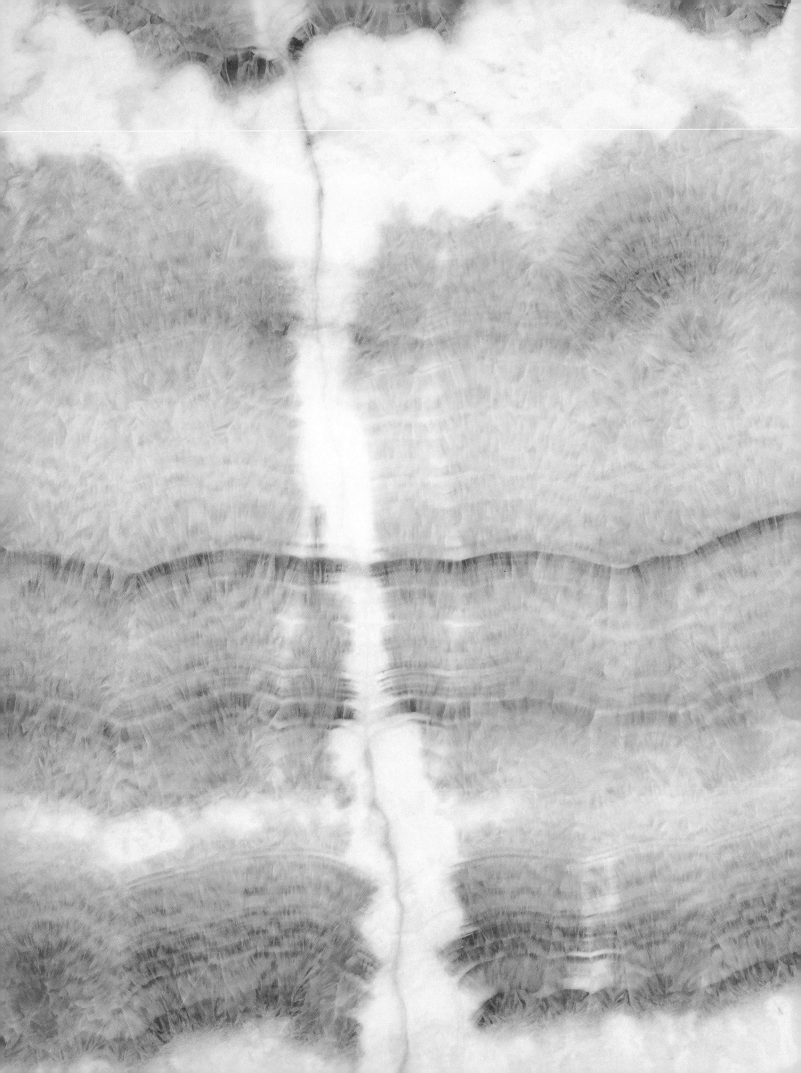

INTERVIEWS
PART ONE

INTERVIEWS

TANGUY VAN QUICKENBORNE

Tanguy Van Quickenborne's personal appreciation for art, design, and architecture has revitalised Van Den Weghe, the marble and stone processing company he took over years ago. Through the discovery of experimental techniques, as well as his collaborations with cutting-edge artists and designers, Van Quickenborne is carving a new path in stone, with more still to come.

Let's start with how and when your career in the marble industry began.
After studying arts, languages, and business administration, I wanted to do something for myself, like take over or start a business. I was open to anything. It was pure coincidence that my father knew the owner of Van Den Weghe, and that they wanted to move on. So I started working for the company about twenty years ago, with the idea of taking over after a couple of years.

How do you find and source natural stone?
We visit fairs and wholesalers. It's a push and pull: we offer new stones, but architects also ask us to find something they've seen. Sometimes particular stones are not processed anymore, but we always keep our eyes and ears open for new marble and stones to offer to clients and architects. I find inspiration in visiting art fairs, artists' studios, cities, churches…

Is there a type or style of stone that you see trending amongst designers?
Firstly, there's the fashionable colours. It started with green and pink, then came yellow, and now blue again. We keep up with those trends and I can somehow feel which colours will be in fashion. Secondly, there's the contemporary and sober designs, with grey, white, and black. Those two trends are always there.

What is your favourite type of marble?
Two years ago, I redid my home and used Breche, which forms when rocks come together after an eruption. Really interesting. I also like colourful stones, like yellowish stones with orange, and I enjoy classic travertine or Carrara.

How do you feel the marble industry has changed over the last few decades?
With 3D technology and AI, renderings are so overly perfect that people expect the results to be exactly the same. Sometimes, clients cannot deal with the fact that the stone encapsulates millions of years of history. They will even ask me to move the marble vein here or there. Nature is so much more powerful than us. Why would you try to steer that into what you want? Natural occurrences are such a nice thing to have in your interior.

Your interest in art has resulted in an extensive collection. Which works of art are particularly valuable to you?
I bought my first piece at the age of 21, for no more than 50 euros. I started with my own generation and as the budget grew, I added works by artists like Andy Warhol and Richard Nonas. I have an Esther Kläs, which I bought from Xavier Hufkens. And a series of works by Darren Bader. He is one of my favourites – the new Marcel Duchamp, I'd say. And I was one of the first people to buy a piece from my good friend Kasper Bosmans about twenty years ago.

What historic work of art or architecture, composed of marble, would you recommend seeing?
Last Christmas I went to the Yucatán Peninsula in Mexico and visited the archaeological sites there. I was in awe of what people did there with such limited resources or means of transport. As for artworks, I'd say Ryan Gander's works are very good, and of course all the classical statues and sculptures.

Lastly, in what way has your passion for art shaped your company?
Van Den Weghe has become more international and high-end, with special projects by artists and designers. The layer we add is about aesthetics, about the connection to art, knowledge of (art) history, and architecture. We also took over a few other businesses in the field – such as tiles and textured paintings – to expand our offering. This is what sets us apart.

JOOST DECLERCQ

Joost Declercq's path into the contemporary art world began at home, under the influence of his family's avid interest in art. Declercq then studied art and worked as a museum director, curator, gallerist, estate director, and consultant, to further understand and explore the meaning and ideology of artists and their work.

Can you share when and how you became interested in the contemporary art world?
It started when I was a student, when I was about 13 or 14 years old. My grandmother was quite involved in the art world and my father was very engaged in politics, but also in literature, visual arts, and theatre. Because my family was so involved in art, I met a lot of artists. They were very good, local artists, but there was this very classical post-war way of looking at art: a square that you put a picture in. And that picture tells you something about the world. Well, that didn't feel like enough for me, I felt that art should be more. So I went to study art history.

Can you share any exhibitions that stood out to you throughout your career?
There are probably three exhibitions that have had a huge impact on me. But one exhibition, 'Westkunst in Koln', curated by Kasper König, was particularly important. That exhibition convinced me that an artist is not defined by an artwork. Art is not about one work, it's about a career.

You recently curated a project that overlapped with the stone processing company Van Den Weghe. How did that go?
I was doing a show in the Castle Marnix de Sainte-Aldegonde in Bornem. First, I analysed the history of the area, which goes back to the 12th century. The fantastic thing is that the castle houses the best private collection of prints by Pieter Bruegel the Elder. In his paintings, you can't always see clearly what is being represented. I was very happy with the project I did with Tanguy from Van Den Weghe and artist Ana Prvački. Prvački made five bee memorials out of marble. They were so amazing in their natural setting: you could see the bees living in the marble.

Are there any current artists on your radar that use marble, stone, or rock within their practice that you find innovative or different?
The work 'All', nine Carrara marble sculptures of body bags by Maurizio Cattelan at the Pinault Foundation in Venice, was quite good. Very often, marble is used just for its beauty. There are not many people who are able, like Michelangelo, to use the beautiful stone and give it a meaning that goes far beyond the aesthetics.

If you could suggest seeing one historic work of art, what would it be and why?
One is the 'Portrait of a Man' by Jan van Eyck at the National Gallery in London. For me, this is the first reflection of the artist looking into himself and asking, 'Who am I?', 'What am I?', 'What am I doing?'. It is one of the most amazing pieces worldwide. The second, which I've seen a hundred times, is 'The Rape of the Sabine Women' by Peter Paul Rubens. The standard of painting is amazing. The composition, the diagonals, the tonality: I don't think there's one painting that even comes close to this quality.

INTERVIEWS

KASPER BOSMANS

Kasper Bosmans' interdisciplinary practice playfully reinterprets modern and historical ideologies into familiar, yet undefined objects and spaces. The artist, born in Lommel, Belgium, currently lives and works in Brussels, and recently completed a year-long residency at Van Den Weghe. Bosmans' refreshing use of marble expands our engrained expectations of the classic medium.

Can you share the moment, artwork, or experience in your life that influenced your path to becoming an artist?
It was like a profile or a life I've always envisioned for myself. I grew up in a very small town. The infrastructures that surrounded me were not answering the profound questions I felt deep inside of me. So I ended up becoming an artist.

The themes, media, and materials in your practice often criss-cross through historical and cultural eras and references. How do you find the elusive topics and characters that are present in your body of work?
The internet is quite amazing. I consult the internet like I consult a book. And whenever I talk to people, I get so many tips and references. Conversations develop and a new field of research or a new focus starts to emerge. I also get a lot of good stories when I travel on my own. Whenever I go to a place and meet someone, we always share a quest.

How would you describe your practice's concepts and ideas to someone who is new to your work?
I gather stories, bring them together, and try to make them into an exhibition that has a texture. If you come to a studio of mine, you'll see lots of samples of textiles, marble, patinas, and glass-blowing techniques. I have a very interdisciplinary practice that is very much based on collaborations with companies, like Van Den Weghe, a hundred-year-old enamel company, or my bronze caster. I use my exhibitions to tell stories and show off technique, but also to convey European stories of pain and identity – but in a seductive, accessible aesthetic. I never felt at home or like I represented my family name properly. Therefore, I never felt like I could reinvent society properly... as a queer and quirky person, or as an artist. But I am a young queer person and I'm trying to claim that space as well.

You've just completed Van Den Weghe's artist-in-residency programme. Can you tell us more about this?
It was so glamorous to get carte blanche to do whatever I wanted for a whole year. It's like something that only happened in the Renaissance, under the Medici. Van Den Weghe has an amazing set of skills and wonderful engineers. It is quite spectacular.

Can you tell us about a work or works produced during the residency?
We made rainbows based on loose sketches. It feels like the opposite of what you would expect in marble as the rainbows display as a light shape. Pleasantly enough, a lot of people who walked in didn't see them as rainbows, but there was a sense of familiarity and surprise. That's what I try to evoke, and I think we succeeded with these pieces. It is a special piece for me, that installation.

When you first began incorporating marble into your practice, what surprised you about the medium?
What surprised me the most is how it works. I had a fixed idea of how marble can be, what it can do, and how it behaves. But it's much more sensitive than I thought. And I'm flabbergasted by the amount of colour that comes out of the earth. Very surprising.

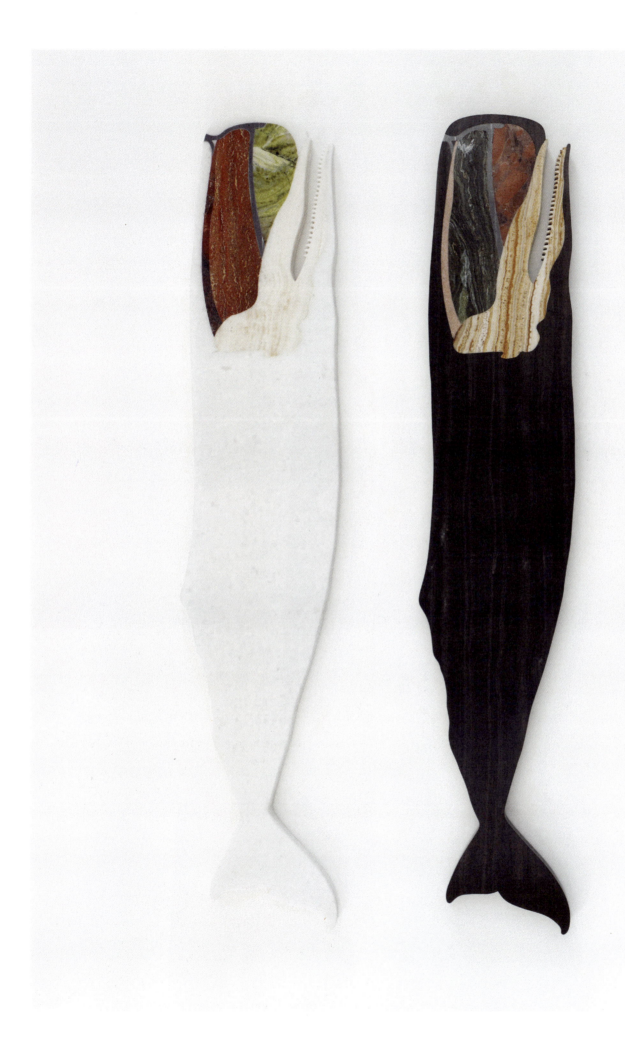

DRIES VAN NOTEN

Dries Van Noten is a world-renowned fashion designer who rose to fame for his exquisite collections composed of colourful prints and flawless craftsmanship. After 38 impeccable years of running the successful fashion brand he built from the ground up, the Belgium-based designer has recently stepped down as creative director. Today, Van Noten continues to contribute to the brand in between his travels and time in the garden.

Can you tell us where you grew up and what pivotal moment contributed to your success?
I was born in Antwerp. My family owned fashion stores and the idea was that I would take over, but I preferred to design fashion instead. My father was quite cross about that, so I had to work to pay for my studies, and built my company all by myself. I was part of the Antwerp Six, which was an informal group of different Antwerp designers. We studied together and managed to put Belgium on the international fashion map. Little by little, my fashion line kept growing. Fashion is very demanding. You have to work like crazy, seven days a week. So last year, I took a step back. I'm still connected to the brand, but I don't design the collections anymore.

When designing new collections, how did nature influence your work?
Nature is very important to me. I live in the countryside and I'm a gardening addict. But when I was young, my father forced my mother and I to work in the garden, which I hated. It was the 60s and early 70s and David Bowie was on the television, which I found far more interesting. But little by little, gardening came back into the life I share with my partner. Fashion is everything a garden is not. For me, nature was an abstract concept that I would then translate into my collections.

Can you tell us about any collections that directly reference marble or stone?
We did a lot of prints that were inspired by marble. It's a technique called marbling where you use oil and water on paper to imitate a marble effect. In the last collection I made, we worked with a small Japanese atelier that applied the same marbling techniques. It was fantastic. That was my last collection: the men's collection Summer 2025, which is now in stores.

The deconstructed marble floor in Galerie Malaquais is amazing. What influenced the store's design and how does marble fit into the overall narrative?
For the stores, we completely adapt to the city and building where they're located. I don't like the idea of having the same stores all over the world. In Galerie Malaquais, we decided to have these big slabs of broken marble, inspired by a friend who made furniture for us. The idea is that you have this counter between the perfect slabs of marble with onyx tops, and the broken marble to simulate a used, antique feel.

In what other ways have you used marble within your home or the business?
My partner and I love marble, so you will see a lot of it in our homes. Antique pieces of marble that were put together again, for example. We also have a marble floor from the 17th century. For the New York store, we're working with a Belgian artist called Ben Storms, who makes huge cushions in the most beautiful marble. Fascinating.

During your career, did you ever experience a creative block? And how did you work through it?
In fashion, you have to deliver four collections a year, so you don't get the chance to have a creative block. Fashion is very strict – it's a bit of a machine. So you have to show your collection, even if you're unhappy with it. The good thing about fashion is that, a few months later, you can start over again.

How do you spend your days after stepping away as creative director?
I'm still involved in the store designs. We're opening stores soon in Tokyo, London, Paris, Brussels, and Milan. And I still advise on the collections. I'm also working on my own project, which I can't talk about yet.

XAVIER HUFKENS

Xavier Hufkens is an internationally recognised gallerist who founded Xavier Hufkens Gallery at the dawn of his career in 1987. Hufkens' architecturally profound gallery spaces have welcomed established and emerging artists from around the globe.

What inspired your decision to open a gallery?
My best friend's parents were passionate collectors of contemporary art, often taking us to exhibitions and openings. Sometimes, artists would even visit their home. I quickly caught the bug for art, and when I turned 18, my parents asked me what I wanted for my birthday. Without hesitation, I asked for a small painting by Walter Swennen, who was exhibiting at a gallery in Brussels at the time. Looking back, it turned out to be a visionary gift, not only shaping my path as a gallerist but also foreshadowing my future collaboration with Walter. To this day, we continue to work closely together. When I started studying law, I spent all my free time in museums and galleries. I loved how art made me feel – it gave me a sense of freedom, both in thought and expression. It didn't take long for me to realise that a career in law would be too rigid for my personality. So, at 22, I took a leap of faith and opened my own gallery in a warehouse near Brussels' South Station.

Can you share a few pivotal moments in the gallery's career that have shaped its success?
Ultimately, what has truly defined the gallery are the artists and their exhibitions. From the start, I wanted to work with the very best. But as a 22-year-old, gaining the confidence of Belgian artists I admired – many of whom already had local representation – wasn't easy. I realised that it was easier to look abroad, convincing major British and American artists to exhibit in Belgium for the first time, which became a turning point. From my first exhibition with Antony Gormley in 1987 to organising the first solo exhibitions of Felix Gonzalez-Torres, Louise Bourgeois, Robert Ryman, and Tracey Emin in Belgium, each of these moments has been pivotal. Another milestone was the recent renovation and expansion of the main gallery by Robbrecht & Daem. The new building marked a significant moment for us, and I hope for our artists as well.

Creating a space and environment where artists feel inspired to exhibit is its own challenge. What is important when designing a new gallery space?
I like buildings with character, but they should never overpower the art. Light and space play a crucial role in creating the perfect atmosphere, and striking the right balance is essential – something that is at the heart of Robbrecht & Daem's practice. In the early 1990s, they first transformed the existing maison de maître into a gallery that felt like home to me. So when we decided to renovate and expand the building, it felt only natural to entrust the project to them once again. I love the interplay of light, the seamless dialogue between old and new, and the way intimacy coexists with the monumental.

Do any of your artists use marble, stone, or rock within their work? How do they approach this historic medium?
Marble, stone, and rock are often regarded as more traditional materials. They were used by the great, masterful sculptors, like Bernini or Rodin. It is interesting to see how, today, these classic materials are used in fresh and playful ways. Take Nicolas Party, for example – a painter with a keen eye for scenography and a fascination with illusion. He often incorporates trompe-l'oeil techniques, creating faux-marble walls and plinths that deceive the eye. He draws from diverse cultural references and questions our perception of materials. But every so often, he surprises the viewer by using real marble, subtly bridging past and present in a powerful way. Another example is Thomas Houseago. From the wide range of materials he works with, one of his signature materials is ash stone, a rock formed from tiny volcanic ash particles. Visually striking and incredibly versatile, ash stone allows Houseago to reimagine sculpture. His approach is yet another example of how contemporary artists reinterpret traditional materials in innovative and unexpected ways.

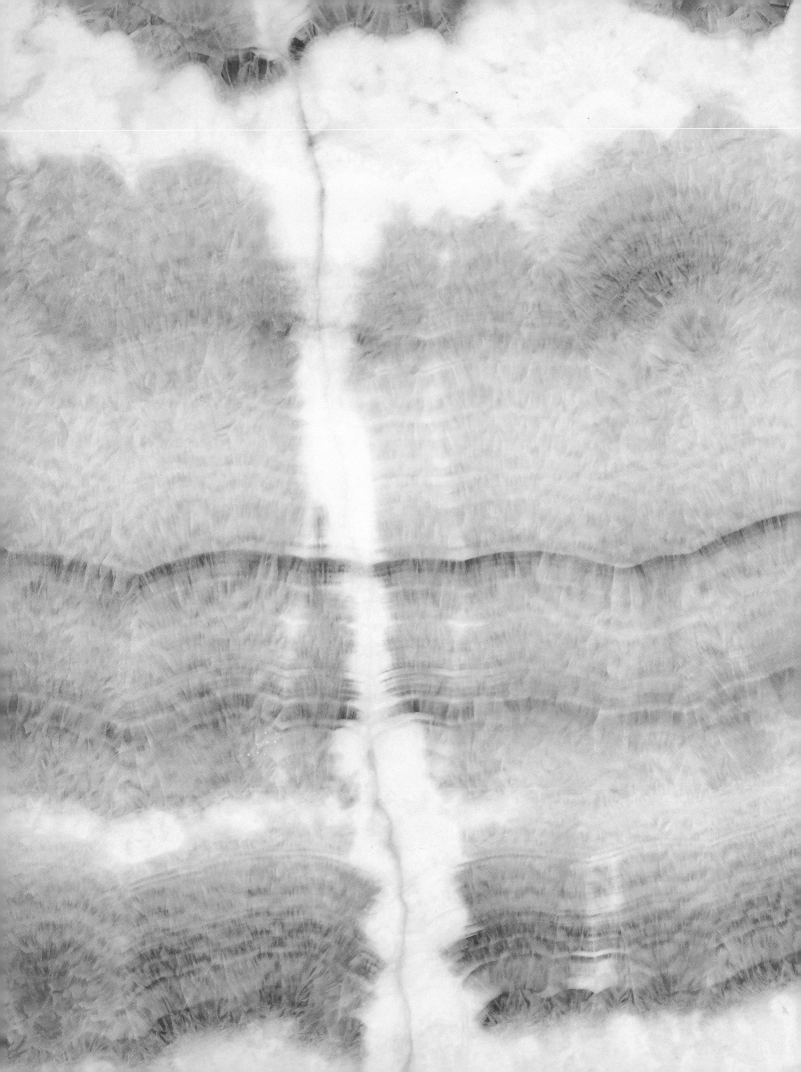

CHAPTER
ONE

CHAPTER ONE

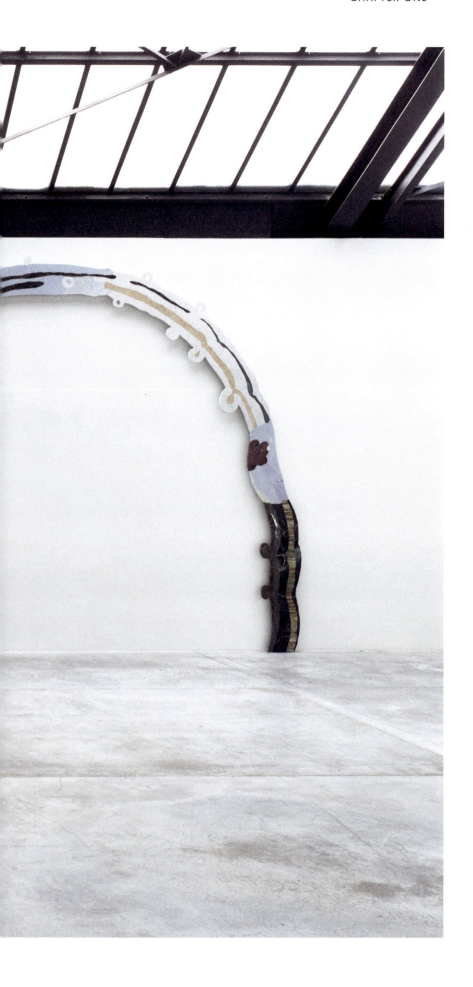

CHAPTER ONE

CHAPTER ONE

CHAPTER ONE

CHAPTER ONE

ROCKED

CHAPTER ONE

CHAPTER ONE

ROCKED

CHAPTER ONE

CHAPTER ONE

ROCKED

pp. 22-27
Kasper Bosmans – Show at CAB, Brussels
Residency at Van Den Weghe, 2025
Various materials

pp. 28-29
Private apartment – Knokke
Design: Grain Design Office
Material: Travertino Jurassico

pp. 30-31
Project VDM – Brussels
Design: Nathalie Deboel
Materials: Florentine Light, Onyx Caldo

pp. 32-35
Project LEM – Sint-Martens-Latem
Design: Benoît Viaene
Material: Crema Macedonia

pp. 36-37
Private apartment – Paris
Design: Willy Rizzo - Obumex
Material: Invisible Blue

pp. 38-39
Private residence – Vinderhoute
Design: Marie-Emilie Geerinckx
Material: Mesh 19

pp. 40-43
Private apartment – Paris
Design: Obumex
Material: Calacatta Macchia Vecchia Borghini

pp. 44-45
Private apartment – Knokke
Design: Grain Design Office
Material: Onyx Ivory

pp. 46-47
Private apartment – Knokke
Design: Grain Design Office
Material: Royal Purple

pp. 48-49
Private home – Drongen
Design: Mathieu Vanquickelberghe
Material: Travertino Titanium Dark

pp. 50-53
Private home – Kruisem
Design: Stephane Boens
Materials: DDS Floor / Carmère

pp. 54-57
Project LVD – Deurle
Design: Marie-Emilie Geerinckx
Material: Verde Patricia

pp. 58-59
Private apartment – Knokke
Design: Joseph Dirand - Obumex
Materials: Grigio Alpi, Florentine Light

pp. 60-61
Private home – Arendonk
Design: Charlotte Vercruysse
Materials: Palladiana Mix Callacatta, Carrara

pp. 62-63
Private apartment – Ghent
Design: Element Architecten
Material: Pietra Dei Medici, Nuage

pp. 64-65
Project DVB – Knokke
Design: Dries De Malsche
Material: Ossidate Bianco

pp. 66-67
Project EK - Lokeren
Design: Jacobsen Arquitetura
Material: Pietra Dei Medici

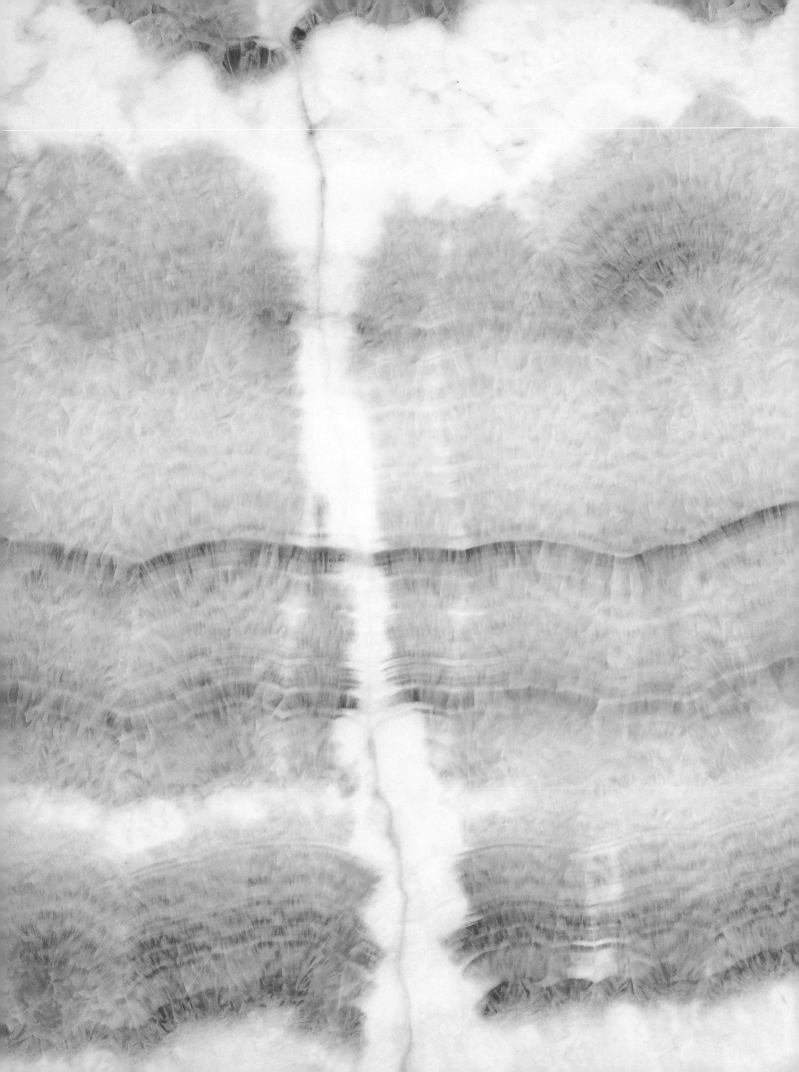

CHAPTER
TWO

CHAPTER TWO

CHAPTER TWO

83

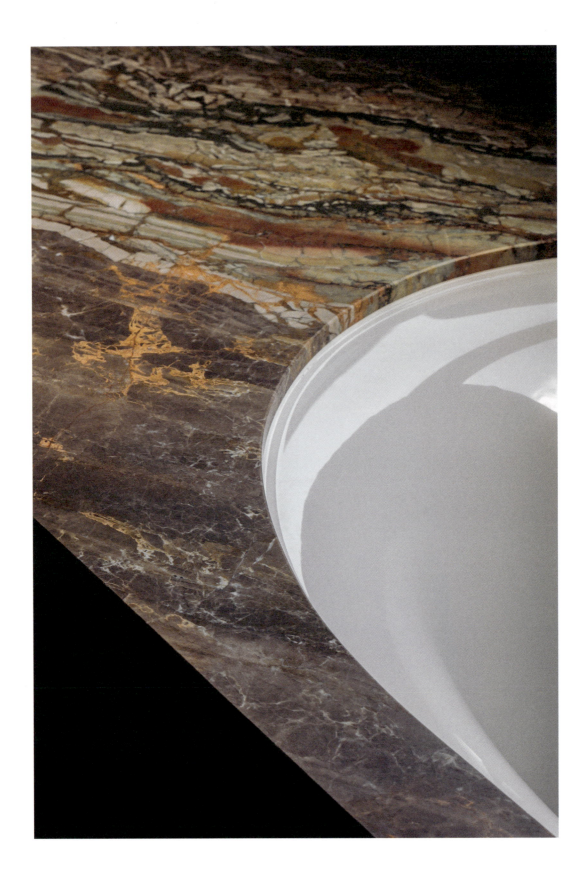

CHAPTER TWO

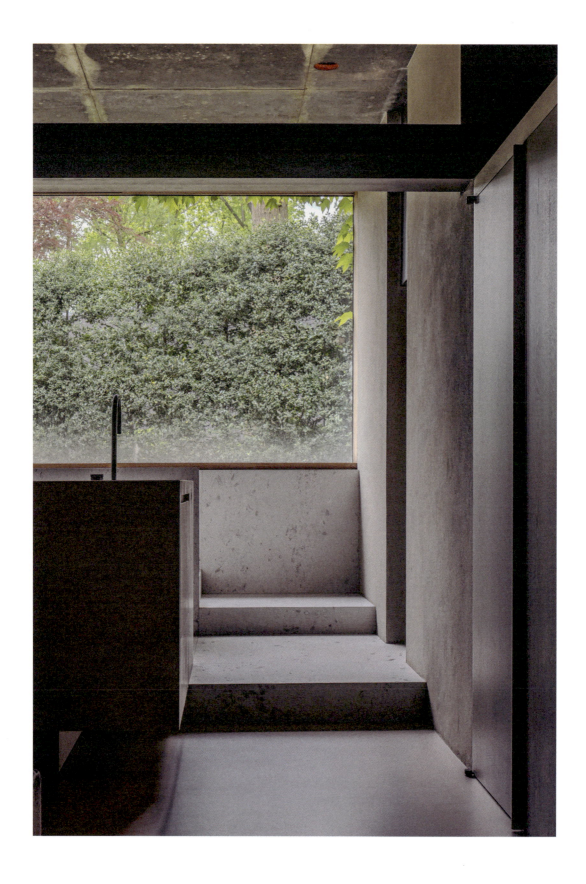

CHAPTER TWO

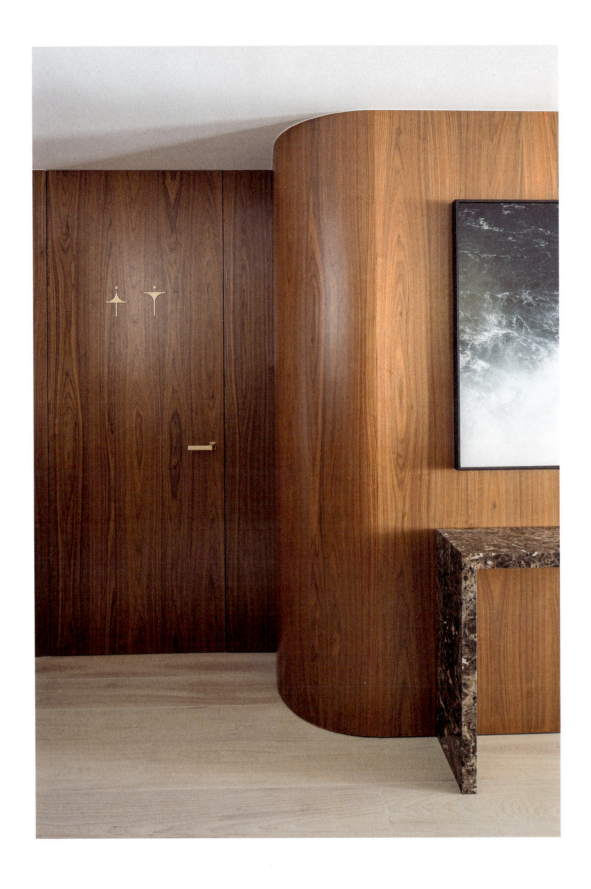

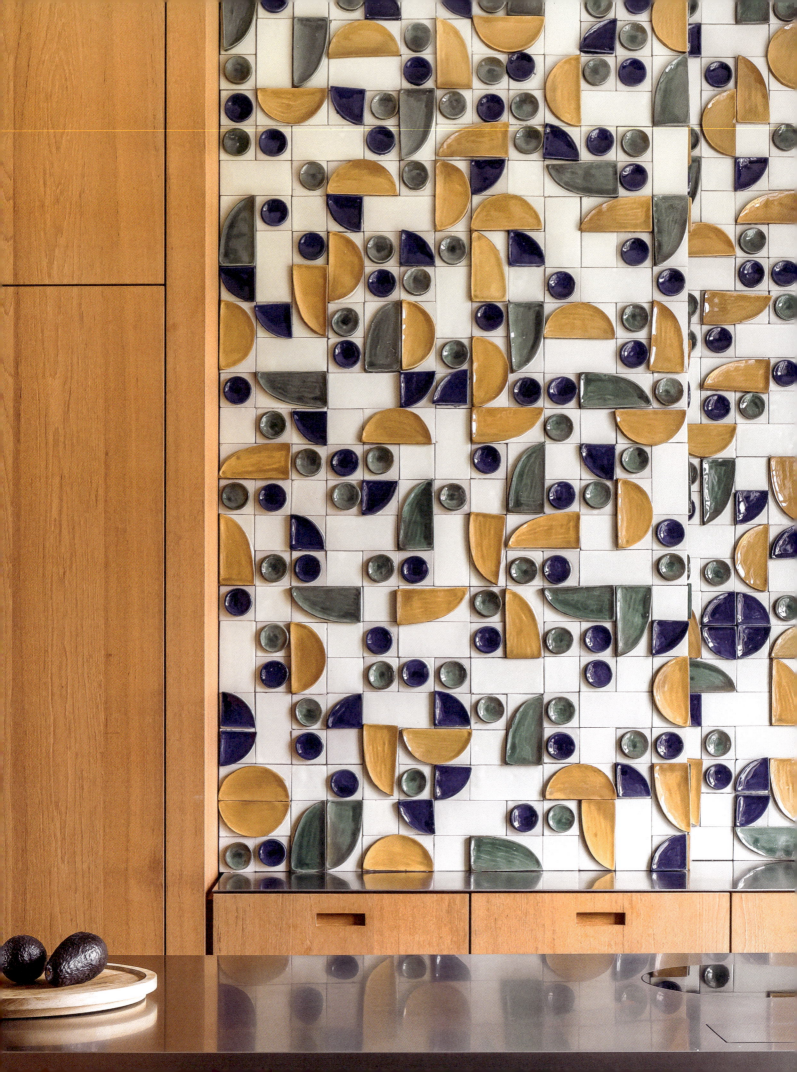

CHAPTER TWO

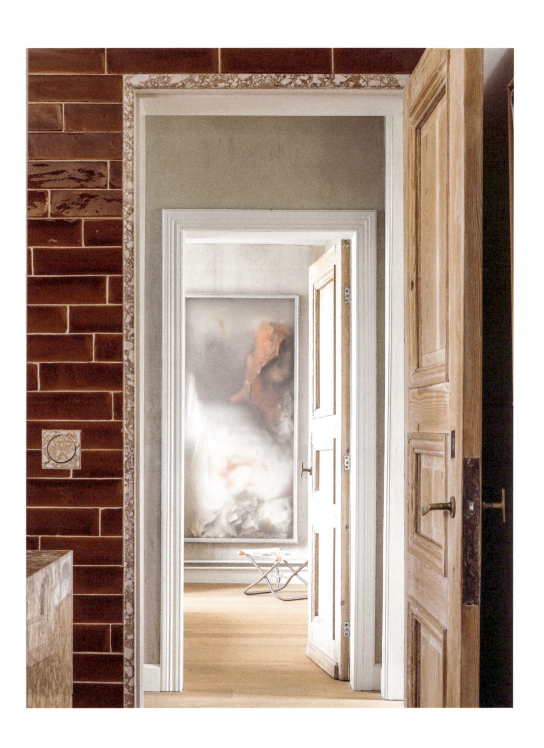

ROCKED

pp. 70-73
Private home – Knokke
Design: Marie Stadsbader
Material: Travertino Classico

pp. 74-79
Project Velasquez – Ghent
Design: Glenn Sestig Architects
Materials: Travertino Classico, Crema Macedonia, Argos Black

pp. 80-81
Private home – Waregem
Design: Wilfra
Material: Travertino Titanium Light

pp. 82-85
Project Sunset – Ghent
Design: Britsom Philips Architects
Material: Pocahodas Honed

pp. 86-91
Project Norah – Deurle
Design: Glenn Sestig Architects
Materials: Stoccato, Crema Macedonia

pp. 92-95
Private residence – Paris
Design: Atelier MKD
Material: Travertino Titanium

pp. 96-99
Restaurant Bablut – Knokke
Design: Pierre Daems
Materials: Emperador Dark, Verde Patricia

pp. 100-105
Project BK – Hove
Design: Benoît Viaene
Material: Travertino Titanium

pp. 106-111
Project VDSR – Deurle
Design: Britsom Philips Architects
Materials: Pocahodas, Sandy Emperador Light

pp. 112-117
Project VQC – Ooike
Design: Frederic Hooft
Materials: Tableau Palmier, Breccia Alicante, Medieval Cognac, Pure White, Medieval Verde, Nuage, Rosso Levante

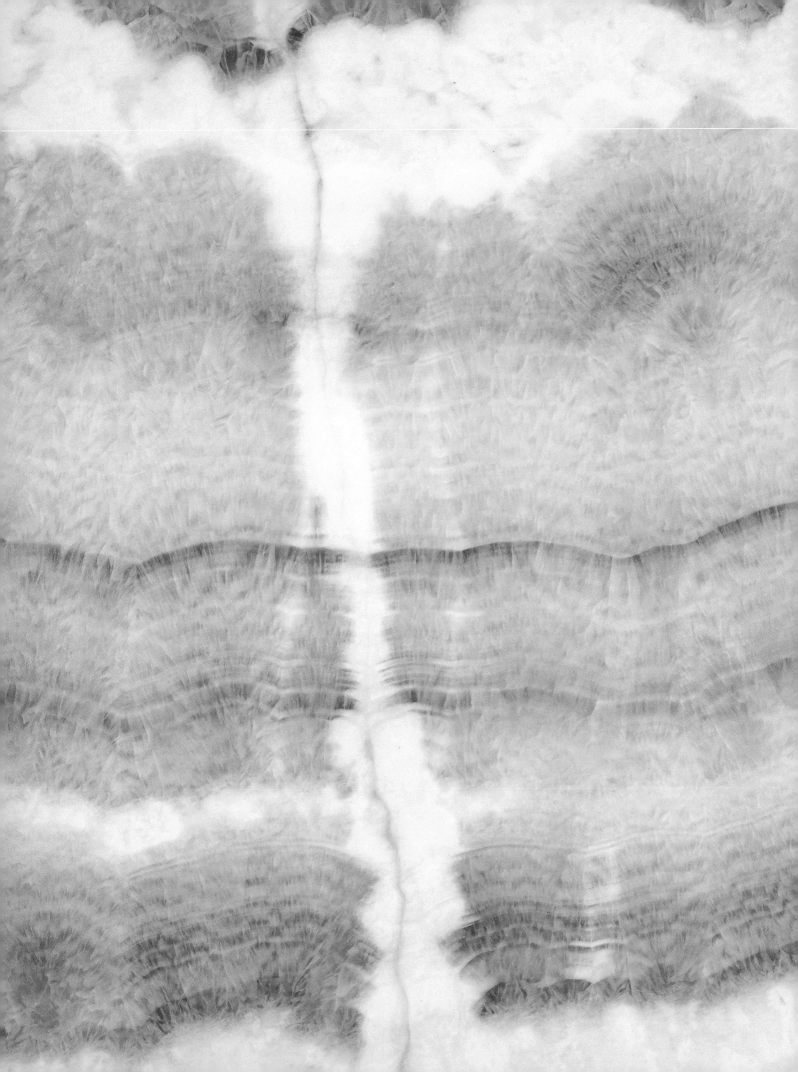

CHAPTER
THREE

CHAPTER THREE

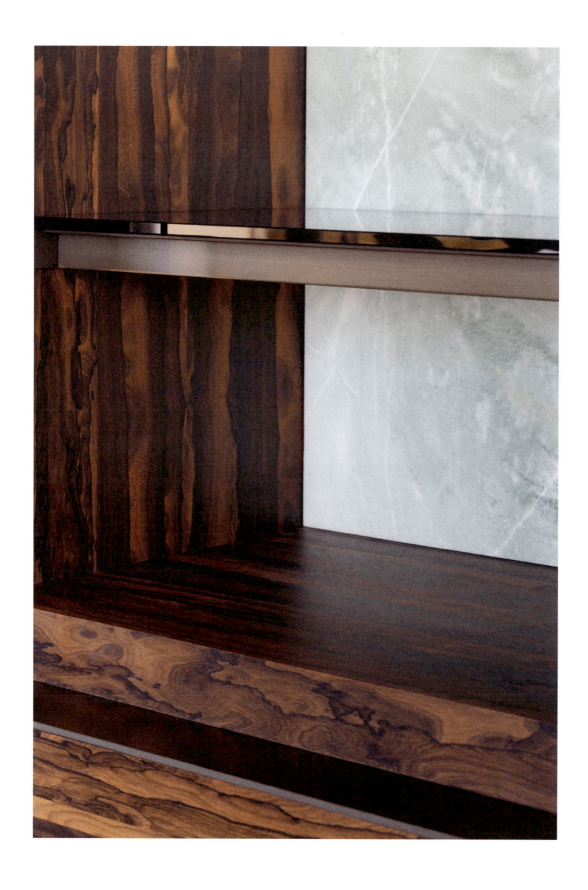

CHAPTER THREE

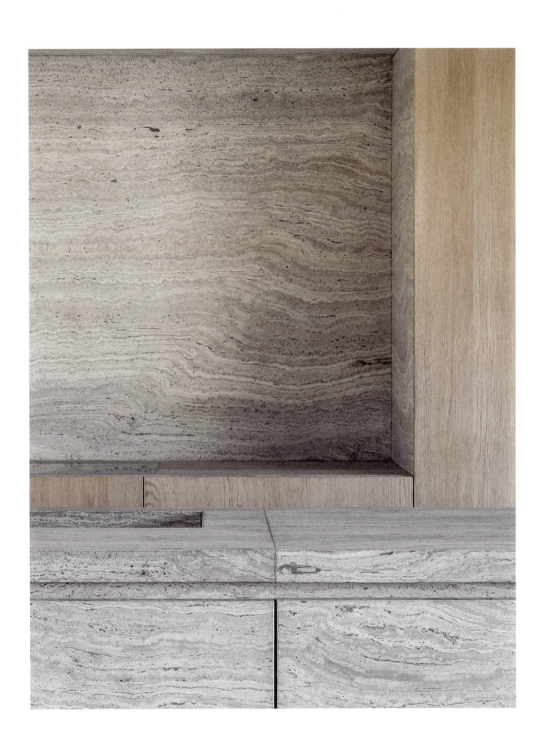

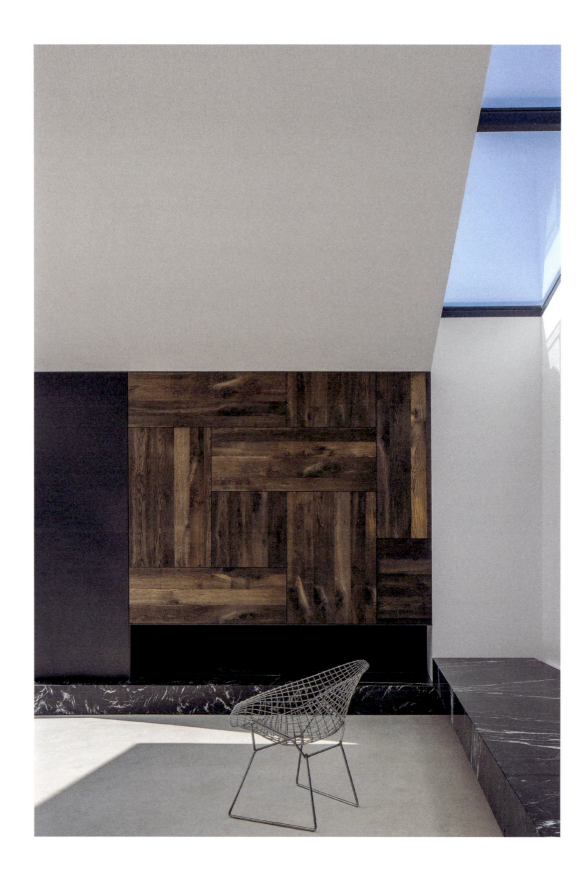

CHAPTER THREE

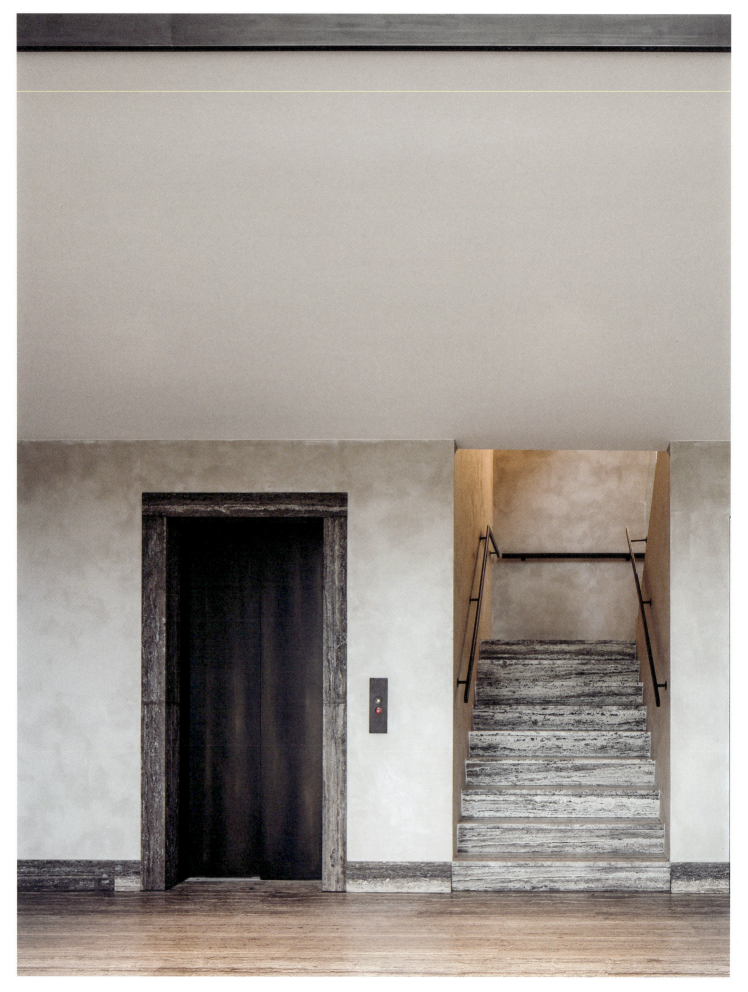

CHAPTER THREE

CHAPTER THREE

pp. 120-123
Private apartment – Knokke
Design: Glenn Sestig Architects
Materials: Travertino Navona, Travertino Titanium, Onyx Jade

pp. 124-127
Private home – Tiegem
Design: Wilfra
Material: Travertino Titanium

pp. 128-129
Private home
Design: De Meester Vliegen Architects
Material: Nero Marquina

pp. 130-133
Baltisse building – Ghent
Design: Stephane Boens
Material: Travertino Titanium

pp. 134-137
Project Caïro – Knokke
Design: Glenn Sestig Architects
Materials: Travertino Rosso, Custom-made Terrazzo

pp. 138-139
Project V. – Knokke
Design: AMTM architecture
Material: Travertino Grigio

pp. 140-143
Project Lina Bo Bardi – Oostduinkerke
Design: Peter Ivens
Materials: Flagstones, Grigio Alpi

pp. 144-145
Private home – Knokke
Design: Charlotte Vercruysse
Material: Calacatta Vagli

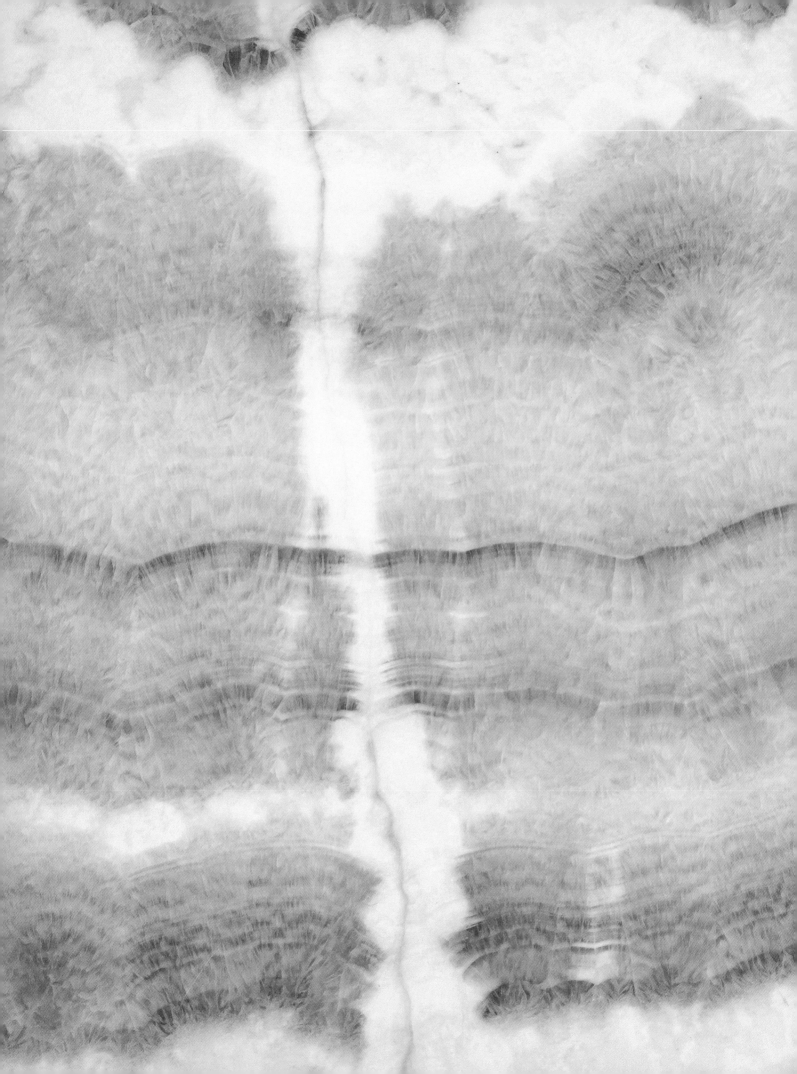

CHAPTER
FOUR

CHAPTER FOUR

CHAPTER FOUR

151

CHAPTER FOUR

CHAPTER FOUR

CHAPTER FOUR

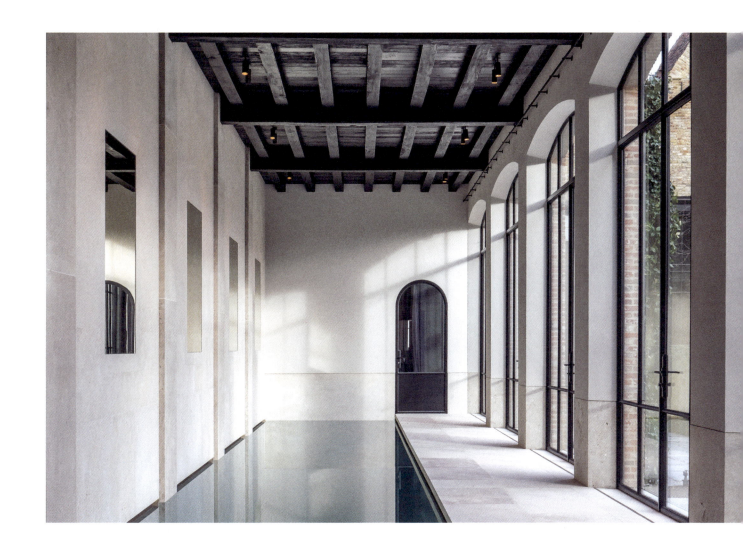

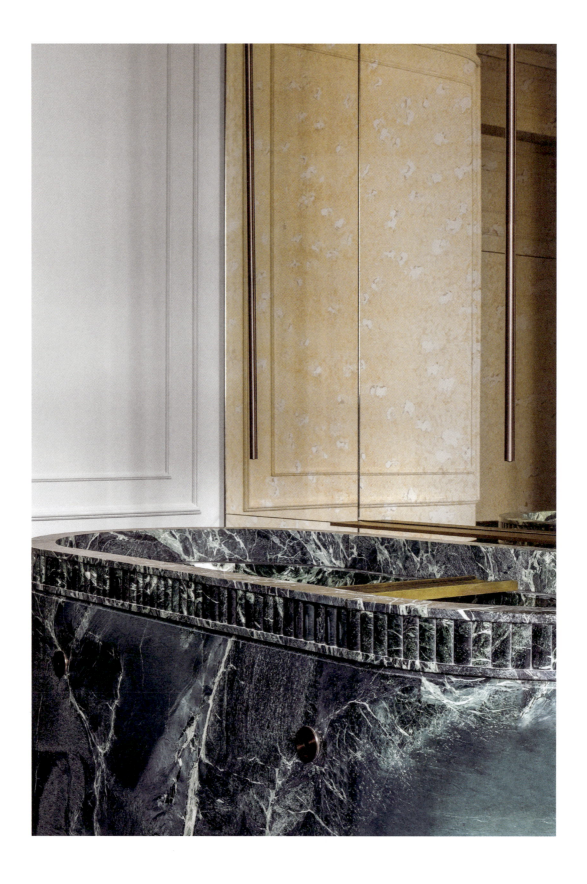

CHAPTER FOUR

CHAPTER FOUR

175

CHAPTER FOUR

CHAPTER FOUR

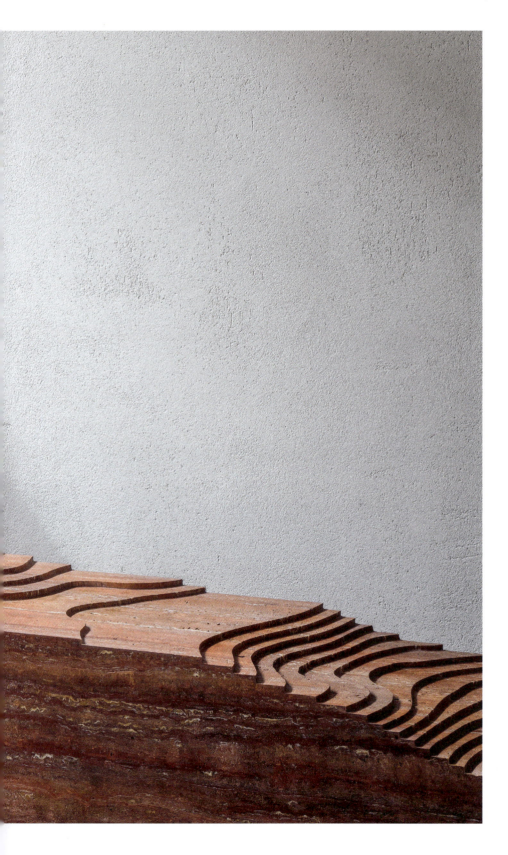

pp. 148-151
The Chocolate Maker
Design: Studio Contekst
Material: Santafiora

pp. 152-153
Project Z.
Design: Nathalie Deboel
Material: Travertino Classico Romano

pp. 154-157
Project TH. – Wortegem
Design: Atelier 10.8
Materials: DDS Tiles, Ispahan Rouge

pp. 158-159
Project MV – Knokke
Design: Marie Lecluyse
Materials: Evora, Pietra Dei Medici

pp. 160-163
Project Leiekouter – Ghent
Design: Stephane Boens
Materials: Didyma, DDS Mosaic, Breccia Verde,
Gris De Liban, Rosso Levanto

pp. 164-171
Project VH – Bruges
Design: Simon de Burbure
Materials: Pietra Dei Medici, Verde Patricia, Onyx Caldo

pp. 172-177
Project DC – Gavere
Design: Pieterjan
Materials: Onyx Jade, Pierre De Vals,
Travertino Grigio, Travertino Rosso

pp. 178-183
Milan Design Week 2024
Hannes Peer x VDW – The Clearing
Materials: Travertino Classico Romano, Travertino Rosso

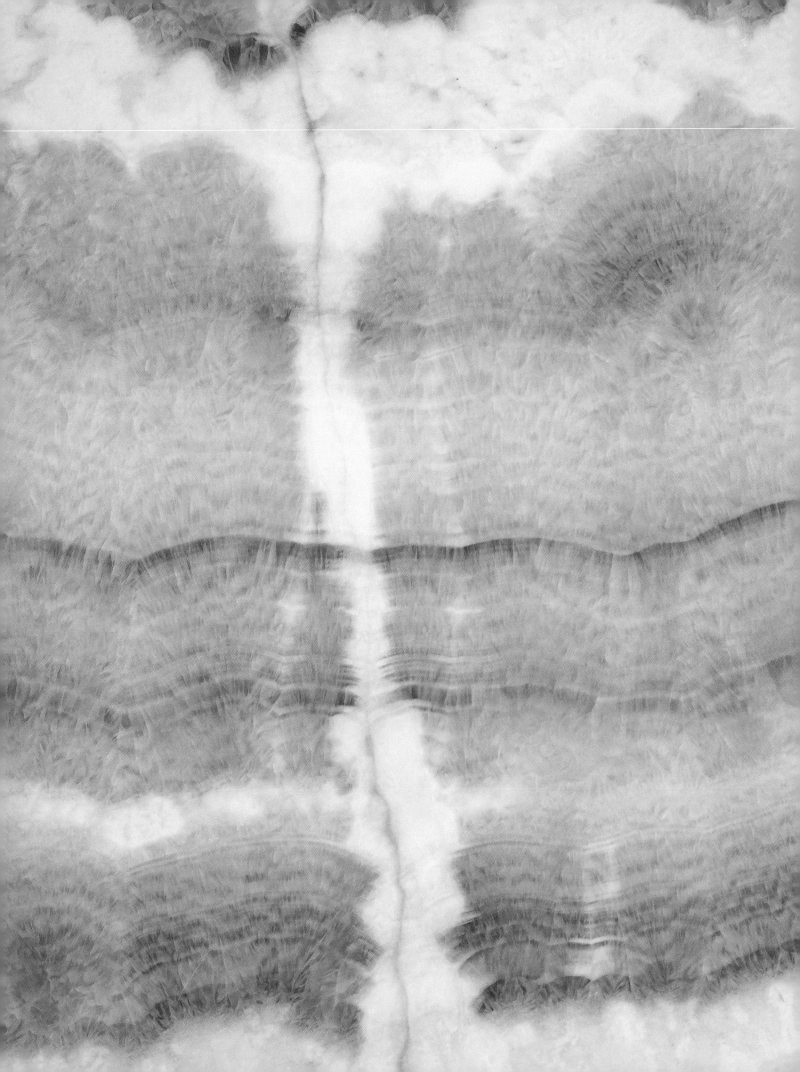

CHAPTER
FIVE

CHAPTER FIVE

CHAPTER FIVE

CHAPTER FIVE

CHAPTER FIVE

CHAPTER FIVE

CHAPTER FIVE

CHAPTER FIVE

CHAPTER FIVE

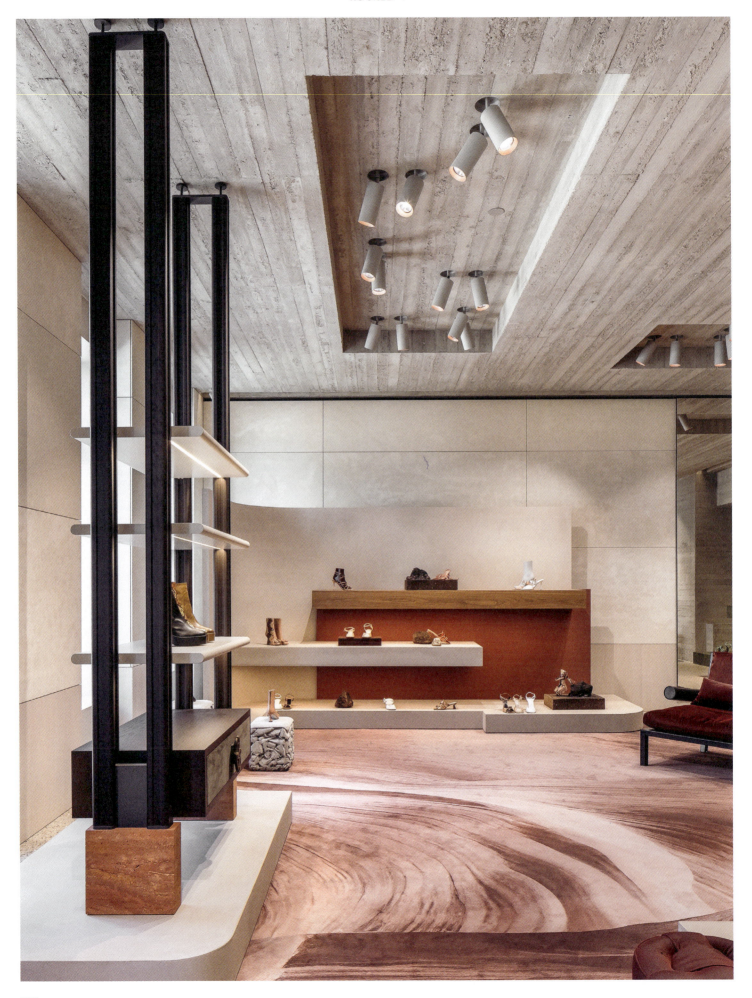

CHAPTER FIVE

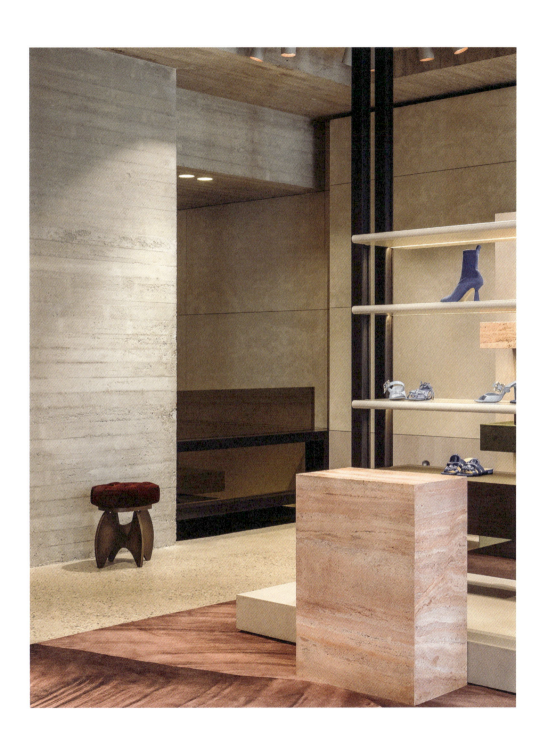

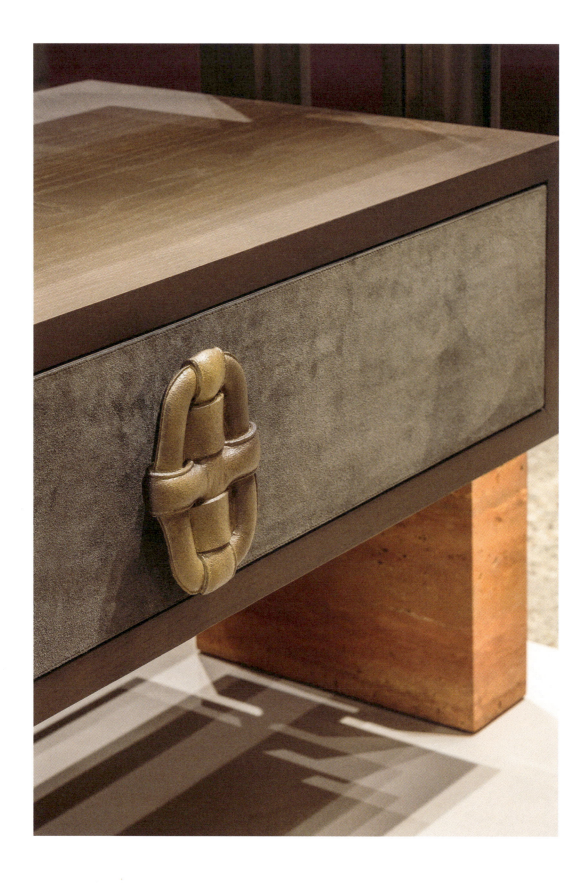

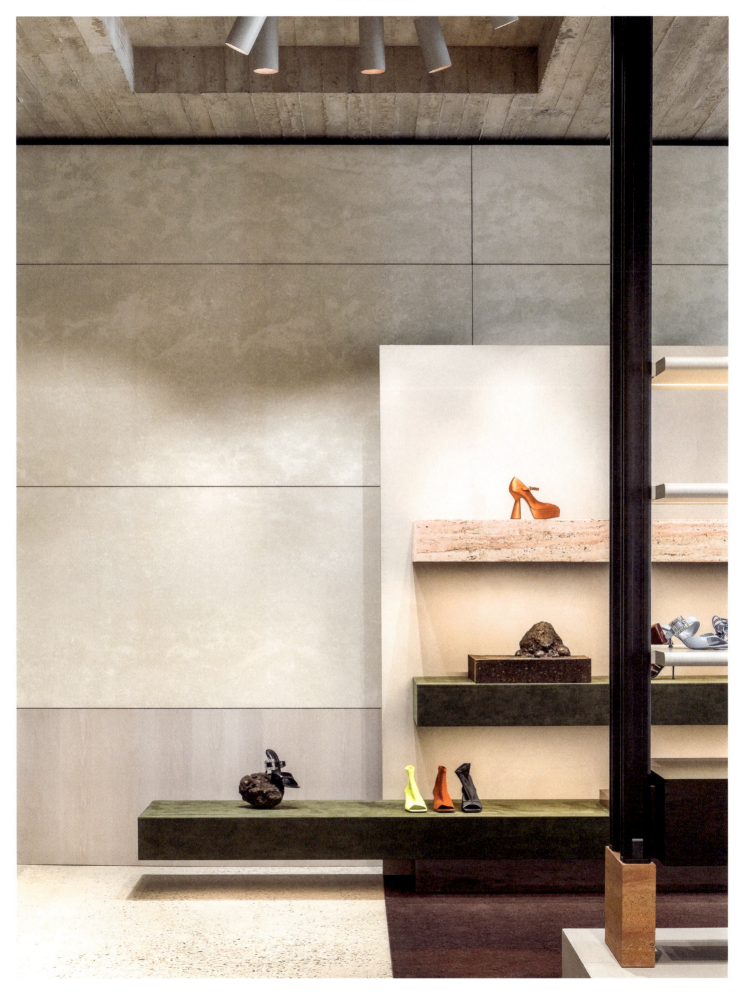

CHAPTER FIVE

217

CHAPTER FIVE

CHAPTER FIVE

CHAPTER FIVE

CHAPTER FIVE

ROCKED

pp. 186-191
City apartment TP – Antwerp
Design: Dries De Malsche
Materials: Travertino Grigio, Argos Black, Breccia Viola, Onazo

pp. 192-195
Dries Van Noten Store – Paris
Design: Gert Voorjans
Materials: Carrara, Calacatta, Onyx Bianco

pp. 196-199
Project P.P. – Antwerp
Design: Linsen Van Diest
Materials: Argos Black, Syrah

pp. 200-205
Restaurant Dunas – Knokke
Design: Grain Design Office
Materials: Belgian Bluestone, Onyx Verde

pp. 206-211
WKA penthouse
Design: Bruno Spaas
Materials: Custom-made VDW Terrazzo, Flagstones

pp. 212-215
Morobé store – Antwerp
Design: Glenn Sestig Architects
Material: Travertino Rosso

pp. 216-221
Project DP – Brussels
Design: Decancq-Vercruysse architects
Material: Muschelkalk

pp. 222-227
CC residence – Portugal
Design: Dries De Malsche
Material: Travertino Rosso

pp. 228-229
The Pink Restaurant – Antwerp
Design: Maister
Material: Custom-made VDW Terrazzo

pp. 230-233
Project Verbruggen – Schilde
Design: Grain Designoffice
Materials: Beige Di Medici, Onyx Ivory, Pietra Dei Medici

pp. 234-237
Residence TL – Schoten
Design: Lieve De Pooter
Material: Breccia Medici

pp. 238-239
Project BL – Antwerp
Design: Dries De Malsche
Materials: Travertino Classico Romano, Carrara

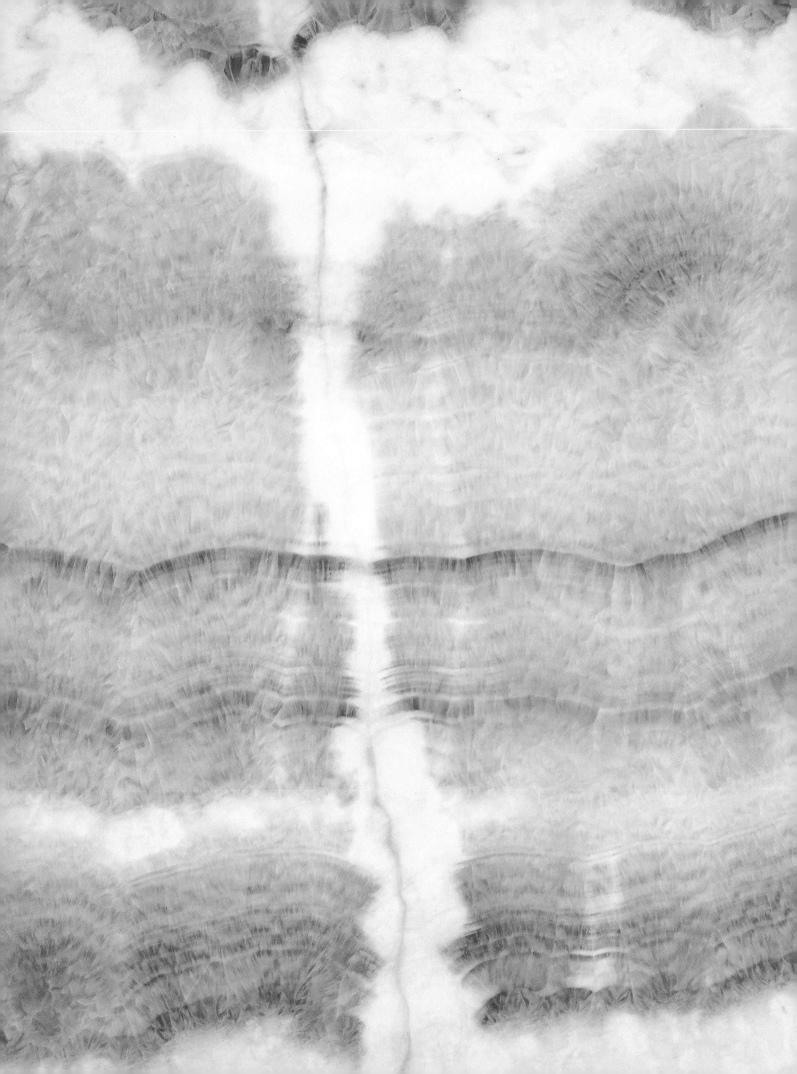

INTERVIEWS
PART TWO

SEBASTIEN CAPORUSSO

Sébastien Caporusso is an architectural and furniture designer based in Belgium. The celebrated designer has crafted a refined aesthetic that speaks to his personal influences and the future of modern design. With a material palette deeply rooted in nature, his timeless mix of materials has captured the hearts of many, and the ambitious designer is far from finished.

First of all, where were you educated?
I studied architecture and design in Brussels, driven by a deep fascination with materials and sensory experiences. From a young age, I have been an avid collector of unique and unconventional objects, each serving as a source of inspiration for my creative journey.

What experience has most inspired your career?
After completing my studies, I moved to Japan, which was a transformative and enriching experience that continues to intuitively inspire my work. Travel remains an integral part of my creative process, allowing me to collaborate closely with local artisans and explore innovative approaches to materials.

How would you describe your aesthetic?
My journey is not a linear path but rather a dreamlike exploration of materials. The tables, lamps, and other curiosities on display represent my earliest creations – transformations of stone, Murano glass, wood, marble, brass, and carefully collected minerals, all crafted by master artisans. This fusion of raw and noble materials gives rise to an unexpected scenography, where eclectic objects and vibrant colours shape my universe. Symbolic forms emerge through organic contours, bold cuts, and strikingly unconventional compositions. I am drawn to rare, irregular, and one-of-a-kind pieces – objects that embody uniqueness and character.

When you want to create a new work of art or piece of furniture, where do you start?
Every creation begins with a concept that is sketched by hand and where the essence of the idea takes shape. I push each concept to its fullest potential, bringing it to life through material experimentation. The most exciting moment arrives during sample testing. This is when unexpected surprises emerge, transforming the vision into reality. As a piece progresses through its creation, the outcome becomes increasingly clear. However, I am particularly drawn to pieces that evolve over time – materials that develop a rich patina, bearing the marks of use and admiration.

And stone is one of those materials?
My material palette is deeply rooted in nature, often incorporating stone, wood, and marble. I integrate these elements thoughtfully, selecting each one based on its unique texture, history, and the dialogue it creates within the composition. Whether as a structural foundation or a refined accent, stone and marble bring a timeless presence to my work, enhancing both its aesthetic and tactile qualities. I greatly enjoy collaborating with Tanguy from Van Den Weghe, with whom I have been working on projects of various scales for several years. Our partnership is built on a clear and dynamic exchange, constantly opening new creative possibilities. It is always a rewarding and inspiring experience.

Where do you go to gain inspiration and new ideas?
Life is fast-paced and intense, yet work remains a daily source of fulfilment, with each day presenting new challenges and discoveries. I deeply appreciate the moments when I can retreat to the mountains for a few days, finding inspiration in their serenity and grandeur.

What are you currently working on?
These days, we are deeply engaged in projects across Southern Europe, overseeing the construction and furnishing of several seaside villas. In Belgium, we are working on a variety of renovation projects, each with its own unique character. At the same time, we continue to expand our furniture line, a growing collection that I take great pleasure in creating.

FIEN MULLER

Fien Muller, co-founder of Muller Van Severen, is internationally recognised for her playful, practical designs that boldly redefine our concepts of furniture, objects, art, and more. Muller's design practice (co-founded with Hannes Van Severen) carefully integrates each material's natural beauty into the narrative of every design.

When did you begin exploring and melding the lines between art and design in your practice?
That really started with the request to create an exhibition together with someone else, who ended up being Hannes. We were renovating our house at the time, which gave us ideas and inspiration. By discovering certain materials, such as brass, polyethylene, and marble, we came up with ideas together.

What opportunities would you say helped propel you to where you are today?
First and foremost was the opportunity to exhibit together with Hannes for the first time at Valerie Traan Gallery. That's where the collaboration started. But for my own work, my studies at the Royal Academy of Fine Arts (KASK) in Ghent were very important. After that, I did a masters in Sculpture at Sint-Lucas Hogeschool in Ghent, which was liberating and made me think about working in 3D and in a more sculptural way. After these studies, I was quickly picked up by a Ghent-based art gallery, Hoet-Bekaert. That's also where we met Tanguy Van Quickenborne.

When and why did you begin working with marble? And what inspired your first marble work of art, 'Marble Box'?
We worked with marble for our very first exhibition as Muller Van Severen. Our first marble work of art, 'Marble Box', are pieces that we still make today. We wanted to use different marbles in a very simple frame, so each box became unique. The different character of the marbles and the different combinations meant that we made very diverse works, but they always had the same simple structure.

Do you have a favourite type of marble or stone?
We often work with breccia viola and also with lardo. These have a lot of drawing and colour and are quite bright and present, which we like.

How do you challenge yourself to think outside the box when drafting new ideas?
It's not easy to explain, as it never happens the same way – there's no pattern. I often draw, and while drawing I come up with ideas, sometimes something small that can create a whole new world. Seeing a colour or material, a technique that we want to master... it's different every time. One idea often leads to another, so we often make families or series. We also call them landscapes. The constant 'open' view in daily life is important in designing our work, not only in a museum or when viewing art, but also at the grocer's or swimming pool. We never stop looking and thinking.

And what does a successful or encouraging day in your studio look like?
A day where you have taken a step – big or small – with the intention to move forwards.

DRIES CRIEL

Dries Criel is a Belgian jewellery designer currently living and working in Antwerp. Shortly after finishing school, Criel launched his own contemporary line of jewellery that charismatically reinterprets how precious stones, gold, and hand-painted enamel are worn and seen.

Who or what influenced your path to becoming a jewellery designer, and where did you learn the craft?
I used to be a ballet dancer and when I unfortunately had to end that story, I was able to find a second passion: jewellery. My goal was always very clear. I wanted to learn as much as I could, in the shortest amount of time possible. I had known how to draw since I was a child, so I just had to combine it with the more technical knowledge of how to make jewellery.
It started with a job at a diamond dealer, and then I went back to being a student at an academy here in Antwerp. I did a diamond cutting course and a jewellery design course, and I'm very lucky to be surrounded by excellent accolades and people that support me.
So along the way, I learned the technical side to making jewellery.

When did you decide to start your own business and launch Dries Criel?
When I turned 25, I had this idea of trying to shake up the Belgium jewellery market. I always had an aesthetic that I wanted to try out and put out into the world, combining it with the classic craftsmanship here. People reacted well to it. My designs are quite specific – very contemporary and with an adventurous character. They are not what you expect them to be, as there's more colour and volume. That's my vision: a contemporary feel and a timelessness in materials.

What would you say is the most challenging part of being a jewellery designer?
You have to always feel what the people on the streets are looking for. Things change all the time. So trying to figure that out without losing my signature aesthetic is the hardest part for me. I want people to enjoy my jewellery on a daily basis, but I still want to trigger them and take them out of their comfort zone. I don't want to make jewellery that feels out of touch. That's not always easy, but I like a challenge.

How do you use marble and stone in your own practice?
I made a jewellery box in onyx, a hard stone, and I use black onyx in my jewellery. I also work with gemstones, like tiger's eye. What I especially like about tiger's eye is that it's very unpredictable. I like the surprise of what the story will be. Will it be darker? Or more gold? Which spectrum will it be, a line or fluid? Every piece is unique, every pattern different. Also, marble and gemstones are wonderful materials. They live, they scratch, they change colour, they evolve – it's never a static thing. They are just very beautiful objects, in stunning colours that are impossible to imitate.

What would you advise someone interested in a career as a jewellery designer to do first?
My advice would be to have a clear vision on who you are as a designer and what you are as a creator, and keep that direction. Bring in something personal because it's the only way to radiate your energy and your story to clients. Otherwise it's going to be much more challenging. Dare to be different. It's not the easiest route. But in my experience it's the best way to start something.

STEFAAN DE CROOCK

Stefaan De Croock is a contemporary Belgian artist whose poetic study of time and our fragility on earth has resulted in an avid use of natural materials, such as marble and wood. His explicit placement of such ageing materials allows each work of art to inherit a piece of unknown history, further exploring how time, earth, and humanity exist as one.

Your current series of works resemble emotional, anonymous figures defined by natural, repurposed materials. What inspired the study of this subject?
I was always interested in patina, because it's an aesthetic imprint of time. For me it's kind of a metaphor: time has an influence on all of us. Time is something we can't really grasp, but you can see it in wood and also in marble. Those materials are also a metaphor, because of the scratches and scars. We all get scarred and have good and bad stories in our life. Losing my brother in 2012 was one of the most devastating moments in my life. I think of him every day. That is why my artwork is shown mostly in a pose, and my figures are a little fragile, thinking, and turned inwards. It takes guts to confront your own fragility and reflect on that.

How do you want your works to interact with your audience?
My portraits don't have eyes, noses, or mouths. For me, it's important that it's not someone specific but a human being. Because that's the story: we are all different, yet we are all similar. If someone connects with the work in an emotional way, that is the most beautiful compliment.

How long have you worked in the medium of marble?
I used it really early on, one little piece. But the most important work was in 2021. I did a show with Bruges Museums. If you look at marble, you're talking about millions of years. I don't think we can really grasp it. It's almost magical. We don't know what's going to happen in the future – no one will remember us, but the stones will be here and they will keep getting formed. I think that's so gigantic. I'm honoured to be able to work with such a material.

How does marble differ from wood when creating your work?
With wood, I'm on my own – I do everything. With marble, it's a completely different approach. I was so happy a couple of years ago, when Tanguy sent me a message and asked: 'Have you ever thought about marble? If you're interested, pass by and have a look.' We had our first meeting and it was so amazing to see all of the stones, their sheer beauty. I quickly realised I needed their expertise to bring my ideas to life. It is an amazing team to work with.

Marble, natural stone, and rock have been used by artists for centuries. What artists working in this medium do you admire?
One of the artworks that I always remember is 'Une muse' by Constantin Brancusi. It's so beautiful. It is a woman, but so refined and re-sculptured. You can feel the elegance in the marble. A contemporary artist is Ugo Rondinone. How he uses stone and adds colour is really bold. I'm always in awe of how he does that.

What is your favourite type of marble and why?
Carrara. It's such a perfect stone to create artwork with. In recent sculptures I used Brazilian stone. It has a high percentage of quartz and I love the texture. It's also a really hard stone, but visually it has a kind of softness to it. I think that's perfect for what I want to show: a fragile human in a hard material.

HANNES PEER

Hannes Peer founded his multidisciplinary design firm in 2009. The designer's thoughtful yet boundless exploration of materials, texture, and colour has brought international recognition and awards to his practice. Recently, Peer designed a series of totemic marble sculptures for Milan Design Week, shining even more light on the designer's prolific portfolio.

Let's begin with what, or who, inspired your career in architecture?
I am an artist's son, which comes with a lot of positive things. How I looked at the world from an early age, my curiosity: this was instilled in me by my mother, a glass artist. So if I'd have to name one person who really influenced my work from early on, it would definitely be my mother.

Which other architects, experiences, and designers have inspired your work or the growth of your practice?
Of course, there is Rem Koolhaas. I briefly worked in his office in Amsterdam. That was a very special time and his conceptual work inspired my work. And in terms of architects, the likes of Frank Lloyd Wright, John Lautner, and Paul Rudolph in New York. Movies are inspiring as well, art, you name it. Everything is interesting to me, because I'm curious about life. My architecture speaks volumes in that respect.

Can you tell us a little bit about the concept of 'The Clearing', your exhibition during Milan Design Week in collaboration with stone company Van Den Weghe?
The title is closely connected to my philosophical research. A clearing is that one spot in the middle of a forest where there is an open area. So we made a stylised forest with sculptures. You move through the sculptures to a clearing in the back, next to a skylight and window. You move towards the light, so to speak. The design concept was all about discovery. There was 'the clearing' inside the clearing, which was quite philosophical, but at the same time really beautiful.

What types of marble were used for these totemic sculptures?
We used travertine, which I love because it's one of the stones that is always a little overlooked. Travertine does not have any veins. It has a beautiful texture and a lot of colour, but you have to get up close to appreciate it. That was why I chose that stone for this exhibition, to elevate the material in that moment. We wanted to work with the thinnest slabs possible, and that is how the whole exhibition took shape. We wanted to show something unique, and that's why I think all the visitors appreciated our exhibition. It was talking about something else, with a more critical view towards the use of marble.

Apart from the exhibition, how do you use or get creative with marble in your own practice?
I love using it in the classical manner. The typical bookmatch is fine – when stone slabs are matched so that their polished surfaces mirror each other, giving the impression of an open book, but I also love using marble on door frames, which is a very Roman thing to do. It's a more historical way of using marble. I love layering as well, in interior design and architecture. And marble fireplaces, which can be very sculptural or architectural, with intricate forms and shapes.

What other types of marble do you enjoy working with?
It is always a conceptual choice. I love lush Arbesscatto marble, Calacatta, and travertine. And one of the most beautiful marbles in the world is Giallo Siena Avorio. I'm head over heels in love with that marble – it's like a Mark Rothko painting.

Photo Credits

Alexander D'Hiet: p. 11
Allard Bovenberg – courtesy: the artist and Xavier Hufkens, Brussels: p. 19
Alohafred: pp. 38-39
Annick Vernimmen photography: pp. 32-35, 36-37, 40-43, 58-59, 74-79
Cafeine.be: pp. 30-31, 54-57, 62-63, 64-65, 70-73, 80-81, 82-85, 86-91, 92-95, 96-99, 100-105, 106-111, 112-117, 120-123, 124-127, 128-129, 130-133, 134-137, 138-139, 148-151, 152-153, 158-159, 160-163, 164-171, 172-177, 178-184, 200-205, 212-215, 216-221, 228-229, 251
DePascuale+Maffini: pp. 60-61, 144-145
FG+SG: pp. 66-68
Jean-Pierre Gabriel: pp. 192-195
Jeroen Verrecht: pp. 206-211
Jules Césure: p. 243
Kristien Daem: pp. 15, 22-27
Marion Leflour: p. 16
Michiel De Cleene: p. 12
Piet-Albert Goethals: pp. 44-45, 186-191, 222-227, 230-233, 238-239
Pilar Shoots: pp. 50-53
Scheltens & Abbenes: p. 244
Sean Van Echelpoel: p. 247
Senne Van der Ven & Eefje De Coninck: pp. 140-143
Stefaan De Croock: p. 248
Stéphanie Mathias: pp. 154-157
Thibeau Scarcériaux: pp. 196-199
Tijs Vervecken: pp. 28-29, 46-47, 48-49
Yannick Milpas: pp. 234-237

Credits

Interviews: *Corynne Pless*
Editing: *Heather Sills*
Book design: *Diederik Serlet – SRLT*

© Lannoo Publishers, 2025
D/2025/45/325 – NUR 450/454
ISBN: 978 90 209 1834 2
www.lannoo.com

If you have any questions or comments about the material in this book, please do not hesitate to contact our editorial team: art@lannoo.com.

All rights reserved.
No part of this book may be reproduced or transmitted in any form or by any means, electronic, mechanical or otherwise, without the prior written permission of the copyright owners and publishers.